UNSOLICITED POEMS

For Zoya

She is contained in all that lies between the first and the last letters of the alphabet, which contains
the original root forms from which…everything in the world [is] compounded.

-Kāmakalāvilāsa

Your name is creation's ultimatum;
To spell it is to spellbind…

Initial Z, the ultimate, buzzes & initiates:
Honey-fed Zeus' usurped thunderhammer
Swings & lightning zigzag penetrates—
Z to O—night's tailbiting zero,
Its petra genetrix pomegranate
Now made gravid with shrapnel,
The many-in-one grenade
Which—O to YA!—expels
The garnet flood, Yes' Dionysian lifeblood

…my Zoya.

UNSOLICITED POEMS

DAVID ROWE

VERNA PRESS

2010

ISBN 978-0-9842281-1-9

CONTENTS

UNSOLICITED POEMS

WALT WHITMAN *IZIBONGO*

Walt Whitman! He who supp'd with the queen & then dumpster-dove for
    dessert!
Walt Whitman! Irrepressible one who did hard time for humping live oaks!
Walt Whitman! He who slept with both eyes open for fear he'd miss
    something!
He who knew the business-end of both a horse's bridle & a bridal party!
He who filled his autograph book with names you never heard of!

Walt Whitman! He whose picture still smiles on the cover of my hard-back
    Leaves of Grass after I inadvertently shellacked it with lawn mower grass!
Walt Whitman! He whose teeth the kids are skipping on the river!
Whose hair is the volcano's capillary lava!
Whose nose is the sundial's gnomon!
Whose nose-grease lubricates the gears of every time piece!
Whose neck is the neck of an electric guitar!
Whose words burst inkpens like temple veins!
Whose beard stuffs the seat cushions of convertibles!

He who procreated in the back of his ambulance!
He who bar room brawled just to see the Joy run red, Walt Whitman!

Damner of torpedoes! Tickler of Hell's bells! He of the cracker-barrel
    cosmology, Walt Whitman!

Walt Whitman! Hirsute patron of the whorehouse who sat the girls on his
    lap & asked them what they wanted for Christmas! Walt Whitman!
    Himself the giver of geological blow jobs!

He who sat up front & talked the bus driver's car off!
He who emulated the holy dung beetle!
Walt Whitman! Who some critics claim wrote only one poem!
Who I say wrote only one letter: O!

YEAR OF THE ROOSTER
for T.C.

Each morning teaches the rooster anew
to forget his fighting spurs, to transcend his lewd
& treacherous designs
in order to fetch for us the divine
light. Thaddeus: with me struggling to redefine
myself as a teetotaling clerk in the death industry
amortizing my bad
karma before the baby arrives
while you gestate in the rehab's in-patient wing,
sap-risin' time the spring's surprisingly impatient:
mortified by its own past, the dogwood nonetheless sports
prepunctual blossoms to coincide with Lent, to relent
-lessly maintain
there's such a thing as redemption,
that it wasn't all in vain
that day we put down
the booze & crack cocaine
to make our way out to the temple gates
where the monks would crown
our awful ache (addiction
both presupposes & perpetuates)
with the stupa of Siddhartha's nacreous cremains
quite as if to reassure us
pilgrims & punks
we're all once or future buddhas.
Oh, & to return to the rooster:
remember: this entire year is rumored to be his.

KANDINSKY'S *UNTITLED #629*, WITH A SHOUT-OUT
TO HOMELESS NAVY VET SCOTT LEE

Let A not equal A
& given that the dame
whose name I don't deign
to recall (no, not at all)
is the subtext of this text,
just as death is the subtext of all life,
it follows that
rather than kowtow to any upstart
joyriding question mark & the spiteful
kitefights of Good Friday, the horizon
done called in
sick with a chartreuse hangover
& if & only if a heart heavier
far than an ibis feather
belies a busterkeaton-esque
googolplex of operatic bric-a-brac,
then & only then is the feasibility of falling
the fuck apart
in a manner at once transcendental &
derby-hatted demonstrated

Q.E.D.

(baby.)

AUBADE

I awaken & then I wait
on my dreams to evaporate.
After a vapid wank, I arise
& wipe the cum from my stomach,
the gound from around my eyes.
I'm pretty ok
the first cigarette, the first couple cups of coffee
of the day
but, from there, it's a bitch: all
I can do is fall
to my knees
&—still in my t-shirt-sleeves—
pray
for that Mercy in which I hardly believe.

KITCHEN WORK

It didn't hit me,
it didn't dawn on me until
I was eighteen & fresh out of rehab
after nearly killing a man,
I was taking a coffee break
before rejoining the West Indian rudies back
on the grill.
It was bankrupt, still
-had-to-watch-your-back
Philadelphia, 1988, not all
that long after City Hall
had firebombed that row house
& let the motherfucker burn,
I had just graduated
from rehab, my first rehab,
where I'd been mandated
after strangling, almost to death,
my college roommate.
The attack was maniacal, all but uninstigated,
& for years, it's true,
I'd blame the movie, *Betty Blue*.
Maybe I had to make him
an innocent victim—
who can say—
but I'd gotten thrown out of school, the one
that only made my father
feel I was too damn good for him,
pleabargained my way
out of attempted murder
charges by checking into the hospital,
& was working the graveyard shift
at the train station McDonald's, the street
people knowing to meet
me in the concourse
at the Angel of Resurrection statue
for the leftover burgers
as we switched over
to the breakfast menu.
It was, as I say,

in the course
of this coffee break
that I'd suddenly remember
the day
ten years prior
when, as my father was out
on a date, his best friend,
that sick fuckin' creep,
had snuck into the bedroom
murmuring something about
wanting to taste my 7UP (or
was it sip my Sprite, for
crissakes?) before
he so gingerly
unzipped me
&
I
in my
terror
feigned sleep.

SATCHelMOuth POem
with thanks to Ken Burns

With BREATH & BRASS
he swings gutbucket alchemy
& hands us back *JASS*
-mine perfume of Story
-ville whores, hemidemisemiquavers
a dizzy My-Cuntree-Tizzathee
pumping his cornet-a-pistons as if
milking the overflowing udders of
EXUBERANCE
                 utterly
                       dry
his cornucopian horn, his kitchen sink
-opated genius
Proclamatin' Emancipation for the REST of us,
a bowler
hat to mute another
As-Below-So-Above
solo so that he conflates
anatomy & astronomy
& herniates the heavens before
laughing a teardrop
from his trumpet's spitduct
onto the wore-out
dancefloor.

MELISMA POEM FOR MELISSA

If to unspool loops of scotch tape
is to generate lightning;
if the right sunlight
makes a celestial alphabet
of strands of vitreous fluid
afloat in our eyeballs;
& cathedral stones
have been known
to come alive
at twilight
& cry out
with birdsong:
never doubt
what sprites may be set free,
what golden honey discovered
in manhandling the beehive
of your name, Melissa:
your orphan-bastard's name, you need
only wield it like a pariah's drum
to succeed
in arousing the sibyl
drowsing within its syllables
until you hear where your true asylum,
that longed-for Elysium, was slumming it all along.

DERVISH DANCE VERSES

Brutally uprooted,
Bereaved of kith & kin,
The reed flute begins to pine & keen
Our cue to unskein, to shed
Somber skin
& widdershins spin our spines

We turn & return
We turn eternal

Of triangular flame the right hand rises,
Aspires to the blameless skies
As the other, water's delta, summons
Virgin ground,
The figures finding consummation
In the crucible of the heart,
Inspired vessel from which we guzzle
Causality's fire-water

We turn & return
We turn eternal

Headstone thus becomes grinding millstone
Becomes ithyphallus
Becomes philosopher's lapis.
With breath for Pegasus
We enter the very center,
Reborn as threshold, the middle pillar
Atremble between the temple's magnetic poles
As our skirts break hyperborean wind

We turn & return
We turn eternal

The great work complete,
All that remains
Is to bring our whirling
Consciousness
Into the city's sclerotic streets.

TORONTO SUMMERTIME & JENNIE COTTON IS HIGH

For now anyhow
Her life's a herky-
Jerky pre-Kitty
Hawk flying machine
Is propelled I mean precariously
By bags of baby carrots,
Her psychotomimetic CD
Collection & non-blinking
Christmas lights on the freakin' ficus tree
For today anyway
Jennie Cotton surrounds herself with attention
-deficit debutantes
& is always ready is Jennie
To squat in the alley
Just to piss
On your fancy epiphanies
For now anyhow
She dreams of a Chateau Marmont
Room of her own
To read Che Guevara in the jacuzzi in
This Cotton prefers chilled vodka to gin
&'d rather be an elegant pedestrian
Than drive some shitbox
Jennie brings out the rapist
In drug counselors & therapists
& when her dog chases his tail, Cotton's
Convinced he's an alchemist
O Jennie Tough & Natural, Soft & Practical as Cotton
Does she contradict herself?
Who *gives* a fuck: Jennie Cotton contradicts herself.

NO CONTEST

On a daytrip into Boston, ostensibly
To rendezvous with Back Bay
Friends at the M.F.A.,
I end up smoking some recreational
Some wreck-all-*Creation*-al rock
In godforsaken Roxbury
Though not before procuring medicine
For the crackhouse hostess'
Spina bifida-afflicted son
(Since baby daddy is busy
With his eyebrows
Polishing the commonwealth's iron,
No parole in Walpole). Between hits,
She proudly produces her E-3
Army dress outfit
All drycleaned, pressed & mothballed
Despite her dishonorable
Discharge. I for my part try to amuse
With the story behind my Tiffany inkpen
Monogrammed with the Muse's
Bitemarks &, following this
Round of n'er-do-well Show & Tell, discover—
As sure as Nemesis follows Hubris—
I've missed the last Amtrak back home
& have to sleep—my poems my only pillow—by the river.
Before boarding the foreboding morning's
First train, I payphone my long-suffering mother
To meet me at Union Station, Worcester, since I'm
Due in court on D.W.I. charges & won't even have time
To change clothes which –she shrieks—*reek of liquor*
&, what's more: I've decided to eschew
Counsel & defend myself
Like, they say, a real man knows how to do.

POEM AT THE RISK OF SOUNDING GLIB

This is gonna show my age but hey:
She broke off a bunch of car antennae
To make me a misdemeanor bouquet
O to be glib about her just wouldn't do
No, it wouldn't be accurate
To get too articulate but hell:
She wore plastic hospital
Bracelets like bangles by Chanel,
Burrs on her trousers for appliqués,
& were I a weaver of Oriental
Rugs this is where I'd shove
The Perfectly Reverent Imperfect Th—read
For it wouldn't be fair
To get too damn fluent
About our affair but still:
The corner catalpa
Would proffer its cigars
Like a proud papa
& find nary a taker until
The day she up & grabs a pair,
Paradiddles the air,
& rimshots the snaredrum moon.

CHEZ COMEAUX ON THE CORNER OF JACKSON

& Rousseau, where the shades
Of Old Hickory & the Sage
Of Geneva shake
Hands:
Everybody's Uncle Lionel insists
On wearing his wrist
-watch on the back of his hand &
Genuflects at the Rock-Ola jukebox
To make Al Green squawk
Like an unrequited archaeopteryx.
Chez Comeaux, Oscar—Big "O"—opts
To yank at his trouser legs & sit at Ms.
Pac-man, fixin to eat him some ghosts.
In his anti-si-godlin pom-pom tam-o-shanter
Haney's on his gaunt heinie with an elegant sufficiency
Of Hostess cakes & turkey necks & High Life
When Miss Clementine, a cabdriver's concubine
With a Nokia for a brooch, sashays her way in
Chez Comeaux & orders a Cosmopolitan
But can't tell poor Frank how to pour it!
All afternoon Fryin Pan's been tellin Big Man
To keep it up & he'll soon be feelin the physics, while fed up
With all y'all's stupid shit,
Billie Jean's front-stoopin it,
Chez Comeaux, down on Jackson & Rousseau.

SHEELA-NA-GIG

Irish iconographers knew
not to dilute the brute impact,
they understood
that to portray hair & breasts,
eyelashes & all the rest, would
serve only to eroticize & distract
from the sublime fact
of her
      gash
that yawning yonic
gorgon's grimace
which doesn't turn victims to mute
stone so much
as swallow our ardor & transmute
its embers
into so much embryonic
                  ash.

¡BOING ES BOING!
for Nicolas

Yes, everything is everything
on an iron dogwood blossom
a colossus moth is resting,
the talkshow host was assassinated
late last night
A vendor wears a backpack
of birdcages like a hopscotch
diagram of chalk
with finches on the groundfloor,
beat-up birds of paradise on top
while the life of his son
depends on bubblegum
In a suit of gladrags,
in a feather-duster head-dress,
an Indian demi-god
dances with a ragdoll,
breathes on her pinwheel & bedizens the breeze
Prostitutes proffer pomegranates As-is,
their phizzes pocked as Toltec basalt,
their teeth as wrecked as Aztec brick
Policletos eat sticky popsicles
en route to breaking up
a scatological fiesta
after a truckload of toilet paper
spills out in the streets
where a bride upchucks
after getting hitched
up in Hiccup Alley
& here goes the jilted *bruja*
with her halo of indentured *chuparosas,*
the toiletseat horseshoe
in her windowsill
altar's still covered in glitter
& broken in two
O like desperate laboratory
mice the mechanic's muscles scurry
up & down his jumpsuit
as he jumpstarts
the hot-rod schoolbus

baptized "Taboo Love"
& the dandified grand-daddy
sits in his parlortorium—the park—
with its cypress tree steeples
& carillon of a million courting pigeons,
picking his teeth with a cactus needle
& surveying the drunken pinking of Saltillo's Sierra peaks.

FOR SIENNA: AN *UNZA-UNZA* SEND-OFF SONG

Like pairs of lucky old shoes
I chuck these
my words after you,
fare-thee-well jujus
in your journey's wake.
Don't neglect to raise up
an I'm a Bum Again, I'm a Bum Again
Hallelujah I'm a Bum Again! cup
before you slake
your thirst at the well-at-wit's-end
& rip down the youth hostel's door
for your open-air dance floor
(this in glorious spite of your
boo-jee host's hostility)
&, in general, persist in your folly & Blakean
shenanigans, for the emptier one's head is
dear Sienna, the more room there is
to invite Grace & Inspiration on in!

BROTHER RAY R.I.P. DAY

While the misguided rest of the nation
Mourned the loss of Ronald Reagan
We sure disturbed us some peace hey
We sure stopped some New Orleans
Traffic in *your* name, Ray:
From out their shotgun
Shacks along the raucous route
Shot girls in haircurlers & slipper-
Shod kitchen beauticians, their men
Pouring good booze
Out onto the streets for you;
Japanese tourists accosted a dancer
Dressed in your obituaries
To learn the import of Tasseled Umbrellas, of Zigaboos;
& kids who knew you
Only as a soda
Pop salesman, a talk show guest,
A singer of ballpark anthems
Second-lined two & three to a BMX
Behind the empty mini
Piano coffin of carnations
& the Black Men of Labor SAPC,
The brass band's tuba essaying mightily
To rev like a muffler-less motorcycle engine until we
All of us ended up
At the Dew Drop
Inn, our funeral parade done
Re-enacting your career's progression
From church to juke joint,
From Sunday Morning back to Saturday Night.

FOR KELLEY

Well she has wet hot
What kind of *what*?
Well she has erotic dreams see about Architecture
& me I'm just waiting to jack-off

She turns the meantime into moonshine
She turns the meantime into moon (I shan't say sun) shine
Nor shall I shun fellatio as too fancy a word
For how she plays
& somehow snakecharms the clockhands

Like a piñata bat her laugh
Her laughter's a new kind of Chaos Theory
O her laughter makes you think of *buttons*
Hers, yours
Shirt buttons, blouse buttons, jacket buttons, skirt buttons
Become for a moment mouths themselves
Mouths atremble with their own secrets & mirth

My shoes alongside of hers
At the foot of the bed
Seem self-conscious
Awkward impostors

Her very nosehairs have *duende*
The circumference of her scalp's got savoir faire
The nipples of her breasts
Demand to be handled
Like castanets!

She takes the four letters
Of the Unutterable Name of God
Stacks them so they make a silly stick man
& takes him in the tub
& teaches him to swim

O I have seen her like I've heard Sam Cooke:
I've seen her stalk to set free
The esoteric bird in burden

& when she stoops to pick a damned dandelion
You immediately understand
How a weed got such a grand name
Or else see the sunflowers forget
How they got theirs
& turn & follow her
In her high-heeled ecliptic
Down Queens Boulevard.

LOVE SUPREME

De-demonizing the spots
between linoleum & wainscot
after yet another of our Brooklyn donnybrooks,
we mean to re-invent the whole premise,
redeem the promise
of our rent-control premises.
Item: harmonica in the turtle tank
(begins the histrionic inventory);
house key as coke spoon;
house plant as scapegoat;
an encryption of boots bottles books
arrayed on the kitchen table,
& Love Supreme's just another ashtray.

HUNGOVER ODE TO MY FATHER

He'll be buried in a borrowed suit my father
Upstaged Martin Luther
& took a poke at the Devil
This in the erstwhile Worcester State Hospital
Between shock treatments & rationed cigarettes &
Made damn sure many years later
To vouchsafe his son
The Devil's pseudonym.

He dropped my mother over the threshold
& that (when she hit the honeymoon parquet)
Was the very moment of my conception I reckon &
Since the divorce his life has encompassed
Broken compass half-way houses & celibate YMCA cots,
Best offer automobiles & limited offer clip & save coupons,
Community Access Cable trophies, afternoon visits with HIV
Positive pantomimes in wheel-less schoolbuses, so many
Sauceless spaghetti suppers with plastic spoons,
Weekly banishments from the Eden
Bar & Grill where the mafia once approached him
For being the most perfectly anonymous
Alcoholic they'd ever seen.

Oh Dad, I've long since learned
To use pen ink which won't run
For my letters to you,
Dad, your half-century like so many synonyms
For son-of-a-sea-cook Sorrow, like fifty
Ironies the Furies have disguised themselves as:
From Army Intelligence to drunken proofreader of how-to books;
From a priori darling of every Denny's waitress
To every-other-weekend custodian of my childhood;
From self-destructive caretaker of churchyards
To telephone-less 911 operator
To tear-assed tilter of pinball games
For want of windmill-armed giants,

Oh Dad,
What is this crazy compulsion of the name
We, Senior & Junior, must share?

LEARNING MEXICAN

We mistake *casas de cambio* for kissing booths
& try & exchange *besos* for pesos
then, in the fishnet
hammock's analgesic embrace,
on the porch of the hacienda
of conch-ensconced brick,
                                   her palms
her palms open
to proffer
a flock
of tiny salty
doves
to be placed
in the aviary
of my mouth
&
this
is the way
to learn Spanish:
from your hosts' 5 year old,
from crowds at the cock fights,
from the local cemetery's cement sarcophagi,
& from your lover
who sends you into town
with an illiterate grocery list
scribbled on a scrap of frond
                              torn from the roof!

FUCK

Man-o-man-o-MAN
All day you struggle all day long
Maybe make yourself a big-ass "Things
To Do" list & get it all done
Congratulate yourself every time you pass
A cantina & don't go in
Pick up a book or 2 at the bookstore
Only to fall asleep that night
& DREAM about HER.

& then when you run into her
Of course she's never looked better
& it's because she's not with you anymore
& it's BECAUSE she's not with you anymore

& Jesus the surfer's teaching her to walk on water, baby
& even walks her dogs

&, after all, YOU dumped HER
Because she cut all her hair
Off & would only wear flip-flops
She reminds you
As if THAT made it any easier.

BELATED REJOINDER TO EDMUND BURKE
for Margaret

There's a curious demand tonight, an imperious personal imperative
to render every moment momentous & covet the O'erlook'd,
to discover the rigger man's passion for the making, unmaking &
    nicknaming of knots,
to take after the Japanese in ceremonializing of all things the placing of
    stones, suicide,
the preparing & serving of tea, or else like Frank & Francine, the elderly
    couple down the street,
who have succeeded through time, love & plain old necessity in ritualizing
    their diurnal runs
across the river in their pigeon-soiled sedan out to the Navy Base for
    duty-free cigarettes,
Frank reluctantly helping to find Francine's canvas Queen of New Orleans
    casinoboat
doorprize of a purse which they both know is to be found hanging faithfully
from the cut glass doorknob in the upstairs bathroom where Frank'll find
    the bath water
still running for their shepherd hound's ever-postponed flea bath which
he'll shut off with a "Shit" that sounds more like a "Hallelujah" every day,
all of which affords old Francine the opportunity to adoringly empty Frank's
    snubnose
of its bullets, & by this time, dear reader, they really *do* need those cigarettes.

O to live in those rarefied realms of the Seismograph of the Soul
where the merest tremor is avidly recorded & evaluated, where every gesture
    enjoys the import
it does when bidding at auction, O to trust that every heartbeat's registered
on some EKG machine somewhere, every fluttering of every eyelid's
    observed
as in monitored sleep, that the Arch Druid's chestpiece quivers minatorily
around the witness' jugular at the slightest untruth, O to emulate the czarina
immortalized in the *Book of Lists #3* for sparing some unknown subject's
    life via
a treacherous comma introduced into her husband's execution mandate,
& hence the appeal of drug-induced Anguish & Stupefaction whereby flipping
    the record album
across the room has become, has finally & formidably asserted itself
as the well-nigh Homeric undertaking it is.

O Monomaniacs & Fetishists everywhere, unite! O George Grosz, I invoke
    thee,
with your fixation for distended temple veins, help me to fashion a varicose
    world!
O Lee Miller & Man Ray, let us establish a semiotics of solarized schaskas &
    bagatelles!
An expired tampon coupon! An expired tampon coupon! My kingdom for
    an Expired Tampon Coupon!
O give me a world of Braille & make of us all joyous, painstaking blindmen!
& you, Edmund Burke, poor hang dog, front & center
for I'm here to tell you just how Vegetables can & must be Sublime!

ON THIS MY BORN ON, MY BIRTHDAY

I awaken to steel pan
Für Elise & the blab of the Brooklyn
Pave, the cross-river Trade Center
Funeral pyre still smoking & me
Still looking for my key
The one to something extraordinary
On this my 32nd birthday.

Eleven-Seven, the day of revolution & election,
Pissing through my ithyphallus,
Yes, micturating through my morning's erection,
I elect to get drunk in the park & see
What I can see in this, the hand-me-down
Brooklyn of Whitman, Henry Miller & Hart Crane
Of ecstatic Slavic brickwork & loophole Hasidic poolhalls,
Drinking Bud tall boys in McCarren Park
& I'm none-the-wiser
On this my birth, my born on day.

WHITE HORSE TAVERN POEM

O Dearly Befuddled,
We're gathered here to-night
To get unwound & unwounded &
As the tavern's supernumerary patrons
We are UNLAWFUL & DANGEROUS
"To those like us: Damn few
& they're all dead!" proposes
Kelley, self-yclept Cutty, who grew
Up in one of those sinister Robert Moses
Tenement houses, aye,
But the ass-end of a firefly
Is not more sensitive to Vitality
Than she
& anon, we're up & gone,
Besottedly stotting round Bleecker
Like two hotly pursued
Antelopes aiming our Ante-Meridian
Amens towards the heaving heavens.

MARGARET

When she's mardi gras manic, Margaret's vocabulary is strictly limited to Sacrifice, Supplication & Scaramouch, to the scrapends of Druidic rain incantations & mispronounced mantras...Gloriously belly-flopping herself into the Mississippi just to displace her ecstatic weight, just to flatter Ole Man River he can still drive the gals bonkers...Getting stuck up in the chimney trying to enhance her impromptu aria's acoustics or was it to better celebrate Blake's chimney sweeps...O she observes every trash day in concocting a Tragic Float from the neighbors' refuse & leading us all in a Tarantella, showering onlookers with pin-holed condoms, soggy match books, copies of the *Divine Comedy* with Paradise torn out...

In the foyer of the dismantled, put up for auction, & reconstructed here in Uptown New Orleans original Eiffel Tower restaurant, a glass & iron vertebra non-sequitur, there reads a placard: Through these very doors passed the likes of Chevalier, Chaplin, Marilyn Monroe &, not to be outdone: Margaret done up as a table-for-two, an erector set rendition of the *Tour Eiffel* serving as tiara, all to apply for a waitressing job...

Big sister to six or seven brothers, she's mad for S.E. Hinton, positively transported by adolescent intrigue, hot-rod rites of passage, stolen kisses atop Ferris wheels; by growing pains, fits & starts & abortions...But how tough to be her child, Margaret taking it upon herself to combine her son's math & music homework in devising an algebra problem that's solved in being played on the fiddle, or else insisting her daughter stop playing & help Mommy find her misplaced reason-to-be, clenching the little girl's wrist so tight she grows to remember it the first time she's handcuffed...

Margaret's got a distinctly Old World aura, like she's done time as a cathouse grimalkin, a Shakespearian also-ran, she pines for hurdy-gurdies & trained monkeys in bellhop get-ups, she recalls handlebar mustaches, skulduggery, mule-drawn trashbarges, Bertolt Brechtian burlesque...O she bolts out of the shower into the streets dragging in tow shower rod & curtain which somehow insinuated themselves into her plaited hair...She toasts with every sip just to justify dashing the glass to the ground, the threshing floor...She's the undisputed Empress of the Unclosed Parenthesis with her halo of question marks & her Story Hat, each charm pendant of which represents a different story: you have only to indicate the dangling cigarette with the burnt filter for instance & she's obliged to drop everything & rhapsodize its Biography.

ANOTHER SPRING

Up to its old hocus-pocus
the New England spring's first crocus
pokes up through the ground
& boldly peeks around for us,
while the leaves of the rhododendron,
my mother's trusty "thermometer
tree," are no longer rolled tight-as-a-reefer.
Just what stains
the robin's breast red, dour Demeter
could best explain.
Soon enough, we'll be hearing
our creaking porchswing's refrain,
the roar of my stepfather's motorcycle, back from hibernation,
& we'll learn what winter's cruel school has taught us, if any damn thing.

ON HEARING FROM MY FIRST LOVE

That entire season in Alaska
even the sun lost its reason
& hung in the sky,
refusing to retire,
as if to eavesdrop on
our young love's intensity.
      Free
on personal recognizance
from the federal penitentiary—
where nights spent guzzling narcotic
cough syrup & tequila with Eric,
my anti-skinhead-skinhead friend from tent city,
had eventually landed me—
I was jumping bail
when she & I parted
those twenty years ago,
when, that is, the Ketchikan-to-Seattle
ferry set sail
& literally parted us,
      our lips,
         as we kissed goodbye.
Sweet as her e-mail
the other day was,
replete with j-pegs
of her wholesome husband & their newborn son,
even some highlights of her landscape architect's
portfolio, right down to her proposal
for how to fill the hole
9/11 left behind,
there was, of course,
no escaping the note's subtext,
her tacit question.
     As a poet's ever got recourse
to metaphor, I'll submit
that our Pacific Rainforest romance
was just too fragile & exotic,
too site-specific, I guess,
for its transplant to the Lower
48 to ever take root & flower.

Or, less
highfalutin, if more self-centered & -incriminating,
it might well be
what the voodoo priestess
tried to tell me
one Thanksgiving Day when
out of a drunken fugue I came to
in the Baton Rouge bus station
& found her staring at me:

I don't know how to handle happiness.

NATALITIAL NOLA POEM

& I just wish
I were poet enough
To do it all justice
& albeit I stuck me beezer
In boo-coo cups of sangria,
I *can* tell you this:
                              'twas the febrile
First of February,
The moon's birthday throwdown
Deep down in the 10th Ward, y'all, & we
Witnessed nothing less than the fuck yes
Palingenesis of Artaud's Theater of Cruelty
Thanks to some second-lining ghetto kids & the public library chess bums.
Talkin' 'bout full-of-mythopoetic-grit Miss Margaret's flaming
King Cake coronation of her daughter, i.e. From She
To Shining She & where were the *Times*
Picayune & Channel 3 anyway
When the Advent of the Chinese Goat
Went down in an Irish Channel alleyway
With a bona fide bon
Fire way past curfew,
Bullhorn singalongs & St. Brigid's blowtop blues
                                        Fuck yes, in*deed*
& the probation officer, he believes I'm still in Chattanooga, Tennessee.

FOR J.C.: AN OVERGROWN HAIKU

I was homeless more or less on purpose—
Ni madre, ni padre, ni perro que ladre—
When we met, you had a home Jennie & yet
Had never even seen it, needed me to locate it
Which I did for half-a-cigarette.
When I confessed to being possessed
By monkey-headed electric eels
You thought I meant metaphorically, I guess
For suddenly I'm in your bedroom
Killing scorpions with a Gucci loafer (no less),
Wearing a divot of crabgrass for a laurel
Crown & ready to work in the fuckin
Hockey puck factory for you, Jennie.
We were engaged-to-be-engaged (I've still got
The e-mails & the scars to prove it), even researching
Foreign canine quarantine laws
But it didn't take long, it seldom does,
Before I went from Byronic Hero
To Moronic Window-punching Drunk.
But what I wouldn't give Jennie
Just to get another haircut from you,
Just to watch my curls
Land on your back lawn
Like calligraphic characters
In a crazy unkempt haiku.

A MILLENNIUM SONG FOR OCCUPATIONS
after Walt Whitman

Even as the carpenter knows his woodgrains & his woodknots
So the machinist knows his metals
By the shower of sparks they give off!

The automotive engineer strives to synchronize
Windshield wipers with the driver's eyeblinks!

The Mexican chicken farmer stuffs empty
Eggshells full of Easter confetti!

The Chinese noodle factory workers
With their altar candles flickering
Through the thick fog of flour!

The anthology editor thinks of himself more as a floral arranger
While the florist fancies himself an anthologist!

The gaffer at the glory hole
Blows glass as if the goblet will
Touch the lips of his best beloved!
While for his bloody lips, the harmonica player
Has a fancy brass spittoon!

With his technophobic cohorts the resident
Worldwidewebmaster's eternally patient!

The atavistic vintner has stuck with grapestomping parties,
Sure they give the wine a happy start!
O here's to the purple underwear of grapestompers
& their accordion accompanist!

The interior decorator with a dozen rooms to work with
Makes each one evoke a different month!

Inspired by old picture postcards
The third world architect
Squats to show his workmen
His cathedral's floorplan

With a stick in the sand!
The industrial architect sure
Is sure he can design a plant
Whose structure mimics the molecular
Structure of the petrochemicals it will create!

The satellite scientist who dreams of just once
Making a billboard or moviescreen
Out of the moon!

The quality control guy at the Waterford factory
Who still delights in shattering
All the imperfect pieces of crystal!

The beat-up hands of the tinsmith
Recall a couple of heroic buffaloes!
Stage hands make soapflake snowstorms!
& the dishwasher understands a fine meal
Begins & ends with him!

The bacteriologist appraises streptococcus
Necklaces under the microscope!
Coprolite specialists study prehistoric excrement!

Cotton pickers welcome the morning's dew
For it makes their bags heavier
On the paymaster's scales!
While construction workers
Consult an air bubble
To tell if steel & concrete are true!

The city busdriver with driving gloves, dry cleaned uniform,
Paper puncher in its leather holster proudly at his side,
He knows his & all the routes, hell yes!

The composer makes his monogram his music's motif!
While the caricaturist sneaks
His daughter's name into every cartoon
So deftly the Pentagon
Uses them to train bombardiers!

The one-time Chanel model
Turned restorationist

Helps give the Vatican a facelift!
While the ex-pro-wrestler's
Up late in his study
In Minnesota's gubernatorial mansion!

The grass & mudstained athlete's outfit,
The bloody butcher's apron!
The coalminer's anthracite eyemakeup,
The clerk's carpal tunnel syndrome,
The roadie's earplugs!

Portuguese fishermen mend their nets
Alongside of women making lace!

The hotel maitre d' installs potted geraniums
At the ballroom's entrance
So partydresses'll sweep up the scent & make
The debutante's entrance all the more entrancing!

Burrs in his picnicking lover's pantyhose
Inspire the inventor of Velcro!

The postman in his pith helmet!
The theater usher with his bowtie, blazer & flashlight!
The journalist with an old bordello's front door for a desktop!

Street vendors hawking tangerines straight from Tangier!
Fake turquoise from Turkey!
Silk cravats from Croatia!
Tawdry Saint Audrey's!

O from the woodworker to the street vendor,
From the glamorous grammarian
To the city clerk with a cleric's devotion,
We're reminded work is worship,
That if our work doesn't satisfy us,
Then we're just not doing it right!

NEW ORLEANS RAG

O New Orleans, City of Convulsions
its flags forever flying half-mast,

the Mississippi poised like an anaconda
forever fixin' to asphyxiate us all,

while lightning flashes
for the gods' cruel scrapbook, O New Orleans,

Heterodox Metropolis
with sunsets so lovely you forget to chainsmoke,

& all the taxicabs are hyperbolic old sedans,
the driver's name on the sides in careful Olde English lettering;

where schoolboys learn cunnilingus
from magnolia blossoms still on the trees,

every French Quarter clown
learned his magic in the Big House,

& Freemasons hide hard-ons
under their lambskin aprons.

Frowzy & forlorn hangs the Spanish moss
like Mother Nature's nylons hung out to dry

& iron balconies perplex
like wickedly complex
wartime codes.

THE CARGO CULT

of my backwards heart
leads me to believe it's all real
simple: just go & hack away
the tall weeds & brambles
to clear the old runway;
next, illuminate
its length with plastic jugs
of lightning bugs;
then, climb into the control tower
of discarded cardboard,
put on coconut shell headphones,
& wait
for her—the young lady
with a precious stone hung from her navel
& portable pedestals upon her feet—
to arrive aboard
the shiny silver bird
with her world's store
of grace & bounty
ready, once more,
to ruin me.

JACK KEROUAC *IZIBONGO*

Jack Kerouac! He who was hobbled by scruples in his shoes & who liked his hats to lack integrity!

He whose heart broke a little more when the Mexican shamans mistook him for a narc!

Jack Kerouac! He whose pocket change spilled out with a racket whensoever he sat down in public!

Jack Kerouac! Abashed owner of messy cruciform erections! Bi-coastal sulker ensconced in some-or-other intermammary sulcus!

Avant-gardist who ended up a backwoods curmudgeon watching *Gilligan's Island* with a beer between his legs whilst he denied paternity & let his mother's cats piss & shit & upend flower pots all over the plush carpet & who, in high dudgeon, sure hated him some hippies!

Jack Kerouac! Who'd'a preferred being a no-name Negro jazzman teahead or a Buddhist novitiate with begging bowl & bald pate or else a cockney pickpocket perfectly fluent in rhyming slang!

He who staggered into the *Bibliothèque Nationale* drunkenly trying to research his ancestry & succeeded only in mucking up primary documents with some French whore's menses!

Jack Kerouac! He who didn't give a fuck "s'long" as he could buy his "next fancy shirt in a Hong Kong haberdashery or wave a polo mallet in some old Singapore bar or play horses in Australian," Jack Kerouac! Who nonetheless was known to sit forsaken, watching the glass of his windowpanes drip!

Jack Kerouac! For whom a book was complete only when he ran out of pen ink!

He whose pauper's stone in Mass-a-two-shits simply says, "HE HONORED LIFE," Jack Kerouac!

THE SKY'S A DINGY GESSO

Just like the gods had lost all
Interest in today's canvas
As into the lackaday
Street staggers my father
With his Call-
A-Priest-I'm-a-Catholic medal
& Timex Twist-O-Flex
Laughed out of another
Worcester pawnshop but hell
He'll black it all out
Come tomorrow
So it's back to the welfare hotel
Where he'll grapple
With several
Doors before finding his own:
It's the one with halfmoons
Drubbed into the metal
By early morning's billyclubs.

WHITE GODDESS POEM #3
for J.G.D.

In order
to realize
it's futile
to resist her,
I need only
look rapt
-ly into her eyes
& there I am: trapped
& tiny,
truly
her pupil.

MEXICO CITY RHAPSODY

Let's get *chupacabra* bitemark tattoos
Cariña,
Let's riot for button-fly 501's
Jeer the phone company's gringo engineers,
Use our share of the one-million-gallons-of-water-a-minute
& see what magic ensues!

Let's devote entire days to things Green:
To avocados, all the Volkswagen taxicabs, & one-third
Of the *loco* flag on the *Zócalo* which threatens
To sweep the soldiers off their feet
When they try to handle her!

The fingers of the old ladies
Are as lovely & wrinkled
As the paper roses they fold
& which we decorated our table-top X-mas tree
In Austin, TX with one year…
                              O let's become street vendors of handmade roses,
Of Barbie doll accessories & marzipan space-ships!
Let's hock stuffed hummingbirds
Like the one Pancho Villa's mistress
Kept nested between her breasts
Like a homeopathic penis! & do our long division
On maguey leaves, our arithmetic on agaves!

Yoga classes for prostitutes!
                              Chandeliers for all city busses!

Disculpe, but those boots are made of what?
"The same thing you're drinking, *señor*!
The same thing those children play with,
The same thing that holds together the scholar's tomes,
The same thing, *la misma cosa, señor*
That Quetzalcoatl came down from heaven on!"

Let's revere the Patroness of Plastic Toys
In her screen-door chapel!

Drink soda pop from surplus colostomy bags!
Wear our soiled pants like proud diaries
& see what magic ensues!

EAST SIDE LOUNGE

Remember that night the moon was sneezing
fireflies & I was in my first suit for the first time
& we hid from all the scrupulators
at the East Side Lounge & vowed
not to leave before our blind friend
performed a jumpstart miracle?
Or that "Don't Bring What We Sell" sign
we won over saying we couldn't if we *had* to
while the flugelhorn's transplant tally-ho!
set plastic cups to trembling atop bottles of Lone Star
like lampshades in an old Pullman car
& there was that deadbeat Dad smoking a Dada cigar
from out a calabash pipe & you taught me
how to augment his Birthday
Bib of Dollar Bills & Harlem Shuffle?

RE: EYEGLASSES, PINK X-RAYS, NAFTA, &c.

Faux tortoise shell or well
-nigh invisible? it all depends
on what you wanna
say, O future scuba
avatar baby! O thrice-great daughter
of the criminal winds!
Yes Austin Texas with its
Yuppies-in-Pickups-
Birkenstocks-&-Sweatsocks aesthetics
always sucked
but to be Care Of
a lesbian gospel quartet
is maybe *too* much! yet
come (what) May
pink Roentgen rays
will again emanate
from y(our) proverbial window
& NOTA BENE
darling: I suggest you adjust
Punk Emeritus Butcher Bag
to Rimshot Bomba Bunny ratio
after the latest NAFTA fiasco
without of course neglecting to lick
your pretty knuckles
before punching your godkid!

SHOTGUN EPITHALAMION

Dear Thaddeus, dear Elizabeth, dare I say
flagpoles are wearing
bloody nipple boutonnieres
in your honor today?
That drunken N'uncle was out on the bayou at cocks crow
angling for the Royal Nonesuch of your trousseau?
That today & today only Gert Town corner stores
are advertising Chore Boy brillo
pads as make-pretend Golden Boughs
or that the Vieux Carré
trash pick-up today, your wedding day,
never seemed so much like a garbageman ballet?

Heaven knows it's hard enough
to justify sitting down & writing a poem nowadays,
let alone one in celebration not only of matrimony
(when everyone's Russian soulmate's
just a point-&-click away),
but also—& let's not prevaricate—
of bringing a kid into this overpopulated
poetry-hostile shambles
of a world, but all of that, dear Elizabeth, dear Thaddeus,
is just what makes them—a poem,
a wedding, a child—so wild, so precious, so noble.

Now, for lack
of a chimney sweep or a hunchback,
let's tug on Jimmy's blond dreadlocks for luck,
pour a few fingers on the floor
for the late Painless Paul
(painless now once & for all),
pilfer Peter Anderson's ampersands—
those emblems of union—&
let your Best Man
take the wheel of the Big White Van
&, not unlike the devout
do with their prayers at that wall in the Holy Land,
we'll all head out
to the Quarters

& stick this shotgun epithalamion
into the Cornstalk Fence
&, Mr. & Mrs. Conti, I daresay give
those poor tourguides
something new to talk about.

WEEGEE POEM

Worcester's forsythia bushes
Are barely in bloom
When forsooth fellah & *BOOM*:
It's "Weegee's World @ WAM"
Where Baby New Year's already
Bottomed out, become a Bowery Bum;
Where with each breath
Brighton Beach lovers
Deplete heaven's wherewithal
& my face (reflected in the glass
Of every framed photograph)
Is an ersatz, a silver gelatin moon
Illuming the 8 million lunacies
Which keep the clown crying
Copyrighted teardrops, mendicant men
Blowing soap bubbles &
Myrtle of Myrtle Street
Doing her Paddywagon Strut.
Meantime the inspired freak
In the cheap seats
Begins…but hold on Mr. Fellig, THIS JUST IN:
This here moon has gotta sneak
Behind a stormcloud & take himself a *leak*!

WEEKEND A-Z

All weekend long:
Buying our lucky firewood from the local coffin makers!
Chasing me from the bathroom after stinking it up!
Dolling ourselves up in
El negrito wingtips, exaggerated earlobes &
Fireflies for finger rings!
Giving each other heart-shaped pubic haircuts!
Hoping to die as beautifully as Brando collapsing
In his tomato garden…
Junior naturalists, we mistake haircombs for mandibles, a leather belt for a crawling
Kingsnake, & a peanut for a locomotive!
Like a mouse's tail your tampon string dangling from your pussy's mouth!
My Vagablond with her Million Dollar Midriff!
Nailclippings on the newspaper like Sunday's tender parentheses!
Oh we partake of both the oak tree's roots, its groundedness, & its branches' commerce with the sky!
Pigeons shit their liquid paper, conspiring with us to whiteout the workweek!
Q to your U!
Radios of the passing traffic like an attention deficit jukebox!
Scars, her signature, her profile, Neruda: all
The lines you know your lover by!
Urban Penny Walks (tails for a left turn, heads for a right)!
Vulnerability is our slapdash Starry Crown!
We had a beautiful childhood that lunch…& then it was
X-rated pastries from the X-rated bakery!
You & I afloat on the Aegean of your pillow:
Zzzz…Zzzz…Zzzz…

TULANE SPLEEN

Circa the gloaming
there comes the gloating,
the (as a former lover
might say) *glamour lighting*
which even as it graces
the campus crape myrtles
& corroborates the live
oak trees' robust glory
nevertheless fails to impress
this coffee-breaking clerk,
these tenure-track crapehangers
& aquabib artists-in-turtle-necked
-residence. Neither will the night's
satin-upholstered moonlight
succeed in stirring or holding
anybody up
in his tracks
from rathskeller
to two-kegger
               & back...

DAMN IS IT NICE

Damn's it ever fun
To be back in Brooklyn
To be on these streets replete
These sidewalks ablush with thick
Brick dust of sandblasted graffiti,
Amidst Polish matriarchs
In patriotic Polka dots
As they comparison shop
For bottles of breakfast vodka
& hum one of the nocturnes
Of Chopin
   Damn
Is it nice to find your girlfriend's
G spot in the G train
Subway stop
     Damn's it ever fun
So come on
With your 7 a.m. jackhammers,
Your leering-40-ounce-beer-drinking
Parkbench platitudinarians,
Your gargoyles gargling acid rain,
       O Brooklyn!

WHITE GODDESS POEM #2

Left to my own vices
I need to mind
I don't wind back
up in central lock-up, y'all
because it's fixin to be
another night where the dread
mare rides *me*
                so hard
                        so ragged
                                so mythically
I'll hardly remember it in the morning
much less her nest
festooned with the viscera & jawbones
of the hapless
yes, I'm left to my own
nightmare & vices
& need to be damn careful
lest I land the fuck up
in central lock-up
                the hospital
                        the grave.

ON THE STATEN ISLAND FERRY

To see the Statue of Liberty
For the first time,
She whispers: *I can still feel you inside of me...*

& flaccid now & breakfasted
It's hard to believe
This soignée young lady
Was throwing her unmentionables
Out on the balcony,
Using her spittle to masturbate me
So that I might striate   her hair with semen,
Maculate it with my cum.

I kiss her cunt lips
& then her everyday lips
So she can taste   what she tastes like   herself

O in & out & out & in   the sexy simplexity
As inspired a monotony
As exhale & in
Till we fall asleep   our bellies pasted together
Thinking how comely
The kid would be   conceived   by a fuck like *that*.

ST. PATRICK'S DAY PARADE

It's raining bed slats & democrats,
Garter belts & green carnations
In the neighborhood!
On parked car hoods
Heads of cabbage thud
& I grab me an odd leaf
& hasten to bobbypin fasten it to my noggin
Like a skullcap
In the neighborhood
Nay, in the Irish-Channel-meets-the-Black-Sea 'hood
A parading cruiser car indeed
Toggle-switch scratches its sirens
In honor of a martyred red-legged slave,
In deference to the patron of Nigeria & Ireland
& since the ritual of struggle
Is our mutual inheritance
& for the sake of the banished snakes
I'm compelled to make my shillelagh
Into a kooky caduceus kundalini
Spine with a rainbow slinky
For astral serpent & plastic pinecone
For mojo pineal gland
Whereupon a giggling black kid in Boston Celtics gear
He gets the big idea &
Smears a keltic warpaint soulpatch
On his chin with cupcake frosting
Ere I can jump on some beer cans
The better to clog-stomp
Unclog the Passion what's in
Our Shanty/Ghetto Hearts
In the neighborhood
In the Irish/Hip-Hop-Hooray-borhood.

TONIGHT IN TORONTO

But *Angel*— "Don't call me 'Angel,'
I'm not the answer
to your prayers!"
But I *love* you— "You don't love me, you're just
a serial monogamist
in love with *love!*" she informs me
                              O she didn't *even*
but Christ
my on-again-off-again is
off again
& I just
made that I guess
inevitable phone call
to my so-called home:
Mom'll be wiring me
busfare,
setting up the army cot
again
in her basement
& locking up the liquor
(but mainly
she's worried 'bout the gaps
in my resume)
"If booze & big boobs
haven't already
they'll ruin you yet, son,"
she says
& I *am* wondering
what I should shit right down
& doo-doo.
                "O LIFE TAKES ALL YOU'VE GOT
                    ALL YOU'VE GOT & *THEN* SOME"
says the bum
resting on her
queen-sized cardboard
here on Queen Street
to paralegals eating falafels

& tonight in Toronto it's true:
even the stars up in heaven
seem to be dragging
their ancient light into view.

ANGST ALFRESCO

As putti piss in the fountain
of the courtyard of the café,
I'm feeling so miserably *precious*,
a reformed drunkard
blushing over his gourd of yerba mate
amongst these boho bozos
with their politicized diets & angst alfresco,
several endimanche Baptist families,
& a Conde Nast
-y couple making the last
of their many goes-of-it.
Will I ever be able
to rise above the primal
could-I-kick-his-ass/would-I-kick-
this-chick-outta-bed level?
Will I never master the mystic trick
of taking self-loathing & idle loafing
& making of them love's Eucharistic loaf?
As putti piss in the fountain
of the courtyard of the Croissant d'Or
& dragon- & damsel-flies do their darnedest
to gather & darn together this piss-poor
lower kingdom's randomness.

ALL I KNOW

is the moon's pretty damn full
& the datura squanders its perfume
like opportunities & we
she & I can never say goodbye
without breaking-up.
                            All I know is you'd never guess
she's got a G-string, a Gee-*zus* string,
a juice-string up in her pussy
& treasures the thesaurus she found in the trash
& how the rest of the city
disappears when you ride on her handlebars
like a diamond ad for De Beers.
                            O *Rose-Rose-Rose*
beats my heart is all I know
& she grocery shops in souvenir shops
because she lives in the CBD
& she bleeds every month with a real heavy flow
& she can't can't can't countenance
me & my lousy   millennial ennui.

BATON ROUGE

Opening up our avuncular host's
Motorboat
On a Baton Rouge, Win-draw-or-lose-iana boat ride
Our eyelashes & anxieties,
My Rough Rider hat,
All *kinds* of shit flying on out,
Ogling the wine's shapely legs & the knees of the cypress trees
When Katherine, little Kay-Kay,
Grabs the radio: "M'AIDEZ! MAYDAY!
                            APRIL FOOLS DAY!"

Hey now
Here's Huey Long's Capitol Building
Diddling
The clitoral
Clouds
&
The de Medici's
Heraldic mace-head
Graces the façade of the ghetto
Pawnshop
Where Dean's
Dean
Of that rambunctious bunch
The dock crew,
His jacket back says
WWJD for What Would Jesus Do
But Drink Him 2 Cases of Lite Beer & Be into Work for 7a.m., Amen!

At Tabby's jukejoint a black man's peeling white
His bronzed ankleboots nailed to the wall
We tip the waitress to see her
Without her
Cheaters
On
When some winsome LSU student wants to know
What the blues means to us
So we break it down for her thus:

70

"You got your consumers of, producers of,
& the *consumed by* the blues, sho'nuf,
Now pass the bottle, Aristotle…"

FOR MY UNBORN CHILD:
AN IN-PROGRESS FAIRY TALE

When your mother called me in
To the bathroom that morning
I assumed it was to plunge the toilet,
To, you know, hear her horoscope
Or dispatch a flying
Cockroach or something.
In her shock, she'd thrown the home
Pregnancy test kit's
Wand to the floor;
I retrieved it & to restore
Its magic
Placed it front & center
On her mantelpiece altar
& lit a quiet candle.

The Red Sox breaking their hex
& winning the World Series; the ex-
Lover, who still bore
A serious torch, threatening to torch
Your mother's used bookstore;
The two of us, your still oblivious
Parents, throwing oranges into the river
The better to honor the lunar eclipse
(& later: a lustrous saliva umbilicus
connecting our lower lips!);
Your lone aunt
Swallowing that near-fatal
Bottle of pills; all the electoral
Turmoil here & in Ukraine;
& then, too, the local hurricane
Scare to which we
Took a decidedly
Golden Bough approach:
Figuring the answer to too much
Water was: **yet more water**
We had us, along with Thaddeus,
A hurricane party
Right on the levee...

Precious

Child: what hardcore
Baraka you've been absorbing
Since even before
Your Lower Ninth Ward conception.

Ivan proved to be
A non-event, nothing
In comparison to hurricane me
For, sad to say:
Neither your mother's amulet of amethyst
Teardrops that truly tore me
Up inside
Nor my 35th birthday,
Not even the bathroom annunciation
Got me sober right away;
& sadder still: your mother,
Still in her first trimester,
Wasn't wrong to dump me.

Now, however belatedly,
I'm trying to trust
In the old
Maxim that putrefaction must
Precede the realization of spiritual gold,
That there's hardly a fairy tale
Worthy of the name that doesn't entail
Its fair share of toil & heartbreak.

But whatever happens, take
This to heart: I had hoped to grow old—
From Niagara all the way to Viagra, so to speak—
With your mother
In short: I loved her
& you, child, were no mistake.

24 AGAINST 1

Shucked & shattered
I sit on the terrace
after showing my ass
to god
feeling in-bloom bougainvillea
my dozing dog's decubitus
the soothing breeze
are, all of them,
wasted on me.

Shanghai'd & shat on
I sit in the *jardin*
heart tendrils
writhing
like an ante-mortem
octopus
& that my eyes must rest
somewhere on some*any*thing
utterly disgusts me

(& then too my self-disgust
disgusts me too).

O all in all
& alack & alas
& at last I confess:

     I'm just not equal
     to the hours of the day.

WINDOWSHOPPING FOR ASHLEY
ON THE BUS NEW ORLEANS-TO-SAYULITA
X-MAS OF '96

For your present, Ashley:

Pocketfuls of the late autumn oaktrees'
Wistful confetti

All the funky pathos of the Projects
Outskirting New Orleans, of the tricycle-
Rockingchair-&-milkcrate cluttered stoops &
Porches & balconies qualified by the season's
Blinking lights & a dog's contrapuntal barking,
The dormant airconditioners all done up
In tinfoil wrapping paper,
Bows of Spanish moss

Maybe I can smuggle you something
Of the little girl's wonder on the Greyhound
On seeing her first Petrochemical Plant at Night
(Is that where the Tooth Fairy lives, Mama?)
Or perhaps you'd prefer
The Laredo, Texas treehouse
Of tumbleweeds
Or else
The busdriver's tieclip racedog (as skinny
& race-ready
As he is sterling silver)?
Or might the motel
Billboard's guarantee
Of "Pennies-per-Z"
Tickle your fancy
The way champagne bubbles do
New Year's noses?

Look: here's toiletpaper & coffee filter angels
Caught up in the arms of cactus farm cacti!
Oh Ashley, here's a sequin gown
Of compact discs
Hanging from the mirrors

Of a hundred Guadalajara cabdrivers!
Maybe we can persuade that butterfly
Fluttering by the tequila bottles
In the roadside bodega
To rest on your shoulder,
Serve as your yuletide brooch!

Oh Ashley, I'll sneak both my eyeballs
Into the toe of your stocking
& you can find them in the morning
& crack them wide open
With a nutcracker & a giggle!

HAIL, HAIL, THE GANG'S ALL HERE!
AT IRENE'S NOT-FOR-PROFIT BARROOM
GREENPOINT, BROOKLYN
OCTOBER 2001

& What the Heck Do We Care
About any weaponized anthrax scare?
& what's more:
Tonight we accomplish what we strive for
With every wretched pitcher of Budweiser
For it's Turn Back the Clocks Night
& Irene the Eponymous in a good-for-business
God-Bless-America dress
Has the honor (like some high priestess)
& amidst our cheers dismounts her ladder-chair
& puts 25 free plays on the jukebox
("That's one for every hour, boys!") & Harpo Marx
Who knew 8 languages but spoke only Bike Horn
He's the place's plaster caricature icon
While Danny the bartender & ex-fighter
Is only a heavyweight contender here
& there's a flirty, frightened bloke dropped to his knee
Beseeching eyedrops from my girlfriend so that he
Isn't red-eyed for the swing-shift at the bakery
& by night's end
We've all somehow agreed
To go fishing this weekend
With some guy Tommy's
Uncle Rocky at Sheepshead Bay—
Provided we don't go & black all of tonight out, anyway.

LAST DITCH LOVE POEM

HONEY: LET'S FORGET OUR TRAGIC LATELY TRAJECTORY
& HAND ME MY FOLLOW-THE-FELLOW-WHO-FOLLOWS-A-DREAM
HAT OF IRISH TWEED SO'S I CAN WEAR IT ON ME BONY IRISH KNEE
& WE'LL GO VISIT THE ADOLESCENT WILLOW TREE
& TIE ITS PLIANT BRANCHES IN TO A TENDER KNOT
& WISH FOR NO MORE HYSTERICS—THAT
& A PRETTY PITBULL PUPPY
& WE'LL BRUNCH ON TURDUCKEN & TIRAMISU
AT EXACTLY THE TYPE PLACE NORMAL PEOPLE GO TO
AFTER REHEARSING A WEDDING.
THEN WE'LL GIGGLE AGAIN—STILL A PARTY OF TWO—
IN THE FREEMASON'S INNER SANCTUM
& DANCE AWAY—IN STRICT 6/8 TIME—
OUR TARANTULA-BITE BLUES & MAROON
THE *NATIONAL GEOGRAPHIC* CREW
SOMEWHERE IN THE 9TH WARD'S DICEY GEOGRAPHY
& MAKE THE STREETCAR SMASH UP PENNIES
FOR YOUR NEXT SEQUIN BRA
& GET ALL THE ORTHODOX JEWS
TO WAVE BACK AT UNORTHODOX YOU
WHILE I LIMP AROUND REGALLY
IN ONE HIGH-HEEL SHOE
AS PROOF I'VE WRESTLED
WITH ARCHANGELS & WITH BANSHEES, TOO.

NEW ORLEANS-*AND*-BUST! POEM
for Martin, in hindsight

Fuck this cozy status quo   the accursed purveyors of
Of course   Needless to say   &   Well, obviously:
I'm'a spend a   seminal summer   in the slums of New Orleans
Gonna move back in   with an ex-girlfriend
& we'll rarify the pain in passion   have us an unabashedly   codependent
    affair

Yes you can keep all this   domestic status quo
I'm fixin' to eat moldy old King Cake   with the gutter punks   of Jackson
    Square
Ride the trolley all day on a single fare   let the schoolkids cut my hair
Toiletpaper the trees & topiaries of the Tulane M.D.   who said I'd never see
    thirty

At thirty-four, I'm thirstier than ever for   that Well at Wit's End
So fuck this comfy cozy status quo
& when you find me People   pissed on & passed out
Just wheel me home in a wheelbarrow
& if you find me   dead on Lower Decatur   just go ahead
& chuck my cadaver   in the nearest dumpster   y'all

ATTEMPTS AT A FRIEND'S EPITAPH

Not even for all the insolence of your slippers
could the world become your Living Room

Andrew I'm sober now
sober enough I think

to flout your family's bogus eulogies;
all I managed at the time was:

                        Something finally matters

Elizabeth borrowed a car &
she & Kelley sang
along with the radio
in the front seats
& I found a pretty tie to wear.

In the vestibule
we heard a crowd's uproarious laughter
& wondered if maybe you'd resolved
to show up after all, crash your own funeral
especially when we were handed programs
with an 8x10 of you on the cover
looking like a clean-cut Rasputin.

At the reception
your mother greeted us,
told me & Kelley that

                    When she found you Andrew
                       Swinging from the tree
              You still had some of the purple dye in your hair

from when Kelley Miss Clairol'd us—
we smiled politely.

Kelley's in Paris now
& me, I'm in yet another suburb of Hades
Elizabeth transferred to Oberlin I think

& this is becoming a Frank O'fucking Hara but

Shit

Andrew

Since you left
I haven't passed out
betwixt *Love Boat* & *Dukes of Hazzard*
&
who's driving that car of yours,
the one haunted by your grandmother
&
is your other grandmother still digging irrigation canals on the farm
in Bermuda shorts & fluorescent sweatsocks
planning her next excursion to some or other holy land
&
those crabs
in pools
on the rocks
of your mother's beach,
do they still search for a home to carry with them everywhere
like me & like Kelley & like you & your slippers Andrew?

You know you broke Kelley's heart
when you pleaded for help
that time
we followed you
in the playing fields,
the trees on the perimeter with their branches
raw dendrites & neurons,
the albatrosses so impossibly white, obscene really
it had just rained
when your eyes looked like they would
oh I don't even know
they looked to be awaiting the excruciating solace
of Jocasta's brooch
or maybe
they just envied the clouds their raindrops
(now I sound like Kelley a little,
but at least you loved her)
&
you paused

&
shot off

With your teargas laugh

Those nights on Johnny's parapet-less roof
I didn't know whether to court or curse out the moon
for its purity
so
I addressed my desperate, half-assed orisons to you,
the star closest it.

Andrew I'd like to throw all the chairs through all the windows
but I go on biting the proverbial 24-hour bullet.

Verily I've known the days
when the phone cord
regardless of the conversation
looks to be infected
with venereal warts
&
I know what it is to pace
till Dawn shows with her bloodstained fingers;
to have the so-called soul specialists
prescribe you Prozac—
yeah, you gots to subscribe to the prosaic

When the lyrical proves unbearable

But
I also know the Trickster to have his many guises
the lone pear begging to be eaten
&
I know him to keep a different clock

An apocalypse without fanfare

to remind us
to again proclaim *Cheesiness* the highest telos:

like that Nat King Cole X-mas album
I've been known to listen to the year round
the record's imperfections

sounding all the world like a woodfire's popping embers
while on the album cover Nat smiles,
merry ole soul,
he's got an electric log fire plugged in himself.

SOME VERSES VS. DESPAIR
for Kelley (if she'll have it)

I happen to hate Poems about Poetry
But look, it's like this:
It's self-expression
Or self-destruction
It's this inkpen
Plus 8 ½ x 11
Versus my Diurnal
Yearnings
To Die.

No food
In my pantry
No girls
Without panties
So it's this
Rough draft
Rather than another
Draft of beer.

O pen & paper
Seem awfully paltry
About now
But if poetry can't get me
Thru tonight—
This *white-knuckle* night—
What good is it anyhow.

DYSLEXIC SEX

You peel off your tube top, use it to kneel on
& with you on
your knees & my penis in your mouth,
my hands can only contradict themselves:
one clutches at your hair, a despot,
whereas the other gives
you a dozen goofy new hairdos.

Passion personifies the pillows & cushions!
Our haywire tongues tongue the goosedown,
deflower the flower vase, deepthroat the delicate shafts
& splendid testicles of the antebellum chandelier
& otherwise scandalize the room's heirlooms!

Or else our antic lust
will make of us
pedantic anatomists:
with your philtrum,
your second bicuspids,
your xiphisternum,
I've about run
out of things to do!

While free from the solemnity of stockings & shoes
our feet get delirious
start reciting Neruda
& clasp each other
more tenderly than any
hands could ever do!

ESTRANGED ANATOMY

Like sentient rocks inside of me, these teeth;
My belly-button, the six-spoked repository of an isolato's cum;
My scoliotic question mark of a backbone;
The V-shaped scar on my right index finger, syllogistic proof
Of the rapport between a child's portrayal of a gliding gull
& the solo flight of a jazz pianist's unpressed collar!

Feet, those hateful horizontal abruptions; & lips,
A pair of unhappily espoused grubs;
These milkless nipples of mine, man's laconic reminder
Of what the seahorses alone are privileged to know.

& then my eyes—ah, what legions have crusaded
To make of them the universal standards of Blue.

FIT TO AWAKEN AURORA HERSELF ARE THESE DRUNKEN

Crepuscular roarings, proof again
& muscular that bourbon
Tastes twice as sweet
Down on Bourbon Street
With its pristine damsels in distress
-ed leather minidresses,
Conventioneers initiating sperm
Of the moment decisions,
&/or maids of honor with their NASCAR manicures
Smoking marijuana cigarettes
As a squeezebox artist endeavors
To play the Shim Shamettes'
G-strings on outdoor clotheslines
Like be-sequin'd notes
Strung from G-clefs.
                    O Day Is Done
Gone the French Quarter Sun,
& the drepanoid moon—a.k.a. Yahweh's
Raggedy cuticle—joins the supernal kitchenmidden
Of dippers big & small, exoskeleton of scorpion
& Orion the Hunter's rhinestone belt
Until Venus, that indecent docent, conducts us back home.

PLATO UNEDITED

It'd be a vainglorious act of violence
To even try & impose order
Onto those 3 weeks with her
But suffice to say: loose giver muffle truce
She packs us a picnic
Of I mean goose liver truffle mousse
That & a dented thermos of Olympic
Committee Gatorade & asks the ferry
Crew which side is port 'cause we wanna be
POSH on our Fire Island excursion out to see
The ocean &, no shit, all the adults with their little red wagons.
Suffice to say: in 3 weeks, 3 weeks & change, our love
Went from Platonic to Plato *unedited*. She suggests we get pre-
Verbal tonight, baby, & next I know I don't know
My asshole from my spinning 1st chakra
But it's *us*, for once, mocking
The fucking kitchen clock, suffice to say:
She sucks cock & swallows as well
As she sucks demon legions from inside of me
& wears her domestic-abuse bruises
Around Brooklyn like so many proud chevrons
Because what we two can do, people,
With an old bamboo
Makes *every*body
               care.

BREAKFAST WITH MARGARET, ST. JOSEPH'S DAY

While daughter Rosie's busy zilling & belly
Dancing to Willie Nelson & son Edmund's
Over in Biloxi ornamental metal & colorguard drilling,
Miss Margaret, roller of left-handed cigarettes, whips up
In her Constance
Street kitchen cups
Concupiscent curds
Like Wallace Stevens, old turd, couldn't even
For a double dollop of 'WOZ
& last night's dreams (not to mention
A toke of the aforementioned)
Inform her breakfast recipes,
& belting, "San Giuseppe, who lives in a shanty
Along the Mississippi, bless us
Lest we cease to write & rhyme!" nacreous
Peggy, crane of *our* hearts, succeeds
In burning the toast a 2nd time,
&, all ergo-a-go-go, does breakfast
Fast become brunchtime.

HER URBAN GARDEN

It's an occasion fit to be feted
When the beat-up *Papa Still Alive*
Pick-up truck arrives
& she greets
The bartered-for ½ ton of alluvium
Replete with corybantics & accordion
Whose frantic mechanics mimic
Transplanted earthworms' own
Undulations. A green bean plant spirals its
Tendrils like ancestral spirits
Inspired to begin all over again.
Close by the compost pile
The Susans' complicit smiles
Belie fat lips & black eyes while
Miss Rose—high heels & open toes & all—
Goes at dogged cats' claw with a chainsaw
Which furthermore shuts up the sycamore
-to-palm-tree-to-sycamore telegraph of cicadas'
Bourgeois gossip & bushwa,
Quiets the quarrel of mockingbird & squirrel.
She sows seeds an unlit American Spirit
Cigarette's width apart; on the stoop there steeps
A mason's jar of tea in the sun & one
Can only liken
Even the parasitical lichen
To so much manna fallen from heaven,
Her garden
To some lovely D.I.Y. parody of paradise.

IMPROMPTU CEREMONY
TO SPEED MY DAUGHTER BACK HOME

In postdiluvian New Or-le-ans
In lieu of Deucalion's stones/earth's bones
At the base of the golden virgin, Joan
I place a magnolia seed pod,
Its various hairy orifices
As if infested with mountain ticks
Swollen on vaginal blood.
This, I need to believe, is how magic
Happens: a heartbroken father piously playing
With whatever remains intact after the flood.

AS RAVEL'S *BOLERO* UNRAVELS ON THE RADIO

Mia's multitasking with thalassic mud mask, oriental
Ornamentals & tumbler of ten-year Talisker;
Masking-tape asterisks on windowpanes
Footnote Old Nobodaddy's disdain;
A Jackson Avenue cloverbed's
The crackheads' dew-bedecked daybed
& dumpsters're painted orange, white & green
Here in Irish Channel New Orleans
Where Slim's playing him some bottle
Cap checkers with Mr. Henry Custom Tailor,
Wooden clothes pins adanglin'
From their cheeks keep score
&—sake's alive!—Miss Thing's wearing
Chanel Five amidst pigeons & pitbulls,
The kids are using portajohns for playhouses
& Mardi Gras beads for jumprope
Whilst a trombonist sits on a standpipe Siamese
Greasing his slide with KY Jelly & Astroglide!

BACK ON THE WAGON

Drawn this morning
to the monument honoring
the Moot
Battle of New Orleans,
here I sit
in Jackson
Square
killing time
ere it
kills me
& I can't even
fantasize
about the women
I see
because— I don't need a tarot
reading to know—
I'd only
ruin their lives.
                    Behold
the alleged
fruits of self-knowledge
courtesy of thirty days' sobriety.

TAKING THE PLEDGE

Today a young friend wrote
To say, "You're a scapegoat
David, not for others'
Guilt & shame
But rather
For all the violence & lust
For life that goes unclaimed."
      I hear you, dear Tim, I do
But Jesus Christ & just the same:
It's high time I dropped
The whole noble rot
Routine, the ruinous thought
That Saturday
Night needs me,
That to succeed
Is somehow to betray
My legacy.
    What I need instead
Is to own this unholy dread
& melancholy which has me abhorring
Myself just buttering the morning toast,
What I need most
Is to secretly nibble on
My pregnant lover's
Brazilian wrist ribbon
To hasten
Her wishes three
While she sleeps
(& while they still include me).

PEARL HARBOR DAY

I buried my father a fortnight ago
& to get quite forthright about it:
his obituary was less than accurate,
his funeral a poignant mess,
even his interment in the Central Mass
Veterans Cemetery ironic
since the army had arguably ruined him.
So, overwrought & addlepated,
I absquatulated,
I took my happy ass
on the bus to Brooklyn
where it's Pearl Harbor Day
& I'm feeling bombarded indeed
by—to borrow from the Bard— Fortune's
outrageous arrows & slings.
I, myself a bearded & doting
goof of a Daddy, though an estranged one;
I, a chronic Alcoholic
who chooses not to drink;
I, a Poet whose pen
has been left
entirely bereft
of amen
& abracadabra:
I can intellectually identify—Oh,
in theory, I'm well able to find
the Isis behind
this, my three-or-fourfold identity crisis,
but not in practice.
No, to know this cross is
in fact to become
my very ladder up to heaven
only makes it
all the more burdensome.

LULLABY FOR AN ANXIOUS LOVER

& some day soon we'll go to Everything's-A-Dollar
Where I'll holler: Anything you like, baby, it's *yours*!

Bored with blond-brunette-&-redhead   kids dye their hair in Kool-Aid mix

Doña Dora doesn't charge us for condoms   as if to give us her blessings

Everywhere we go they take us for tourists   (we're so lost in love)

Like seagulls at the city dump   you miss the ocean

Your sweet potato pies convince   the atheists amongst us   to say Grace

The neighborhood cobbler's looking for an apprentice

A divorced woman lives in a house   haunted by a benevolent ghost:
She gets home from work & there's a bubble bath awaiting her

Instead of a trio of decrepit wisemen
There was a double-rainbow   the day you were born
& it snowed in Santa Cruz

On the 3rd your mother's retroactive SSI check arrives

Little girl gymnasts are the super stars of Romania

& often enough front entrances   resemble arms   outstretched to greet you

When clouds burst Mardi Gras Indians run for cover
Like ghetto flowers that can't get wet

The doctor has me on a strict diet   of nasturtium blossoms & edible panties
& at yoga class they're gonna teach me to breathe   & bend my way
Out of the mess I've made

It took an acorn top   (Peter's ersatz kiss)   to save Wendy's life

Yes   Lifesaving Kisses & Kwanzaa pies   Little Girl Gymnasts & SSI

Seagulls at the City Dump   Kids with Kool-Aid Coiffures
  & Everything's-A-Dollar
Hush now honey   put your ear   to the pillow & you'll hear
  its heart beat...

SALAMANDER; OR, SPLITTING THE WORD ASUNDER

To get out of its way
& let the word have its say;
to allow salamander,
with its ballistic tongue,
to speak as it were
for itself...

ssssSeethes forth from between
parted lip-flesh the steam,
the humid heat,
to hiss the wheel, the *salamandala*, into motion.

Sa: natural exhalation
made conscious mantra
via the Tibetan lama's
art & concentration;
seed syllable born ready to spill
& to spell its semen-antics.

Sa-*la-illaha-illa-allah*-mander

Sal: first step of the blessed meanderer,
samana en desultory route to salvation;
Philosophic salt, it aggravates
our thirst for experience, which is to say: heartbreak.

Saltatory salmon of wisdom which
puts fire in the poet's belly,
the Promethean liver, iron-rich
& ever nourishing the birdsoul.
Then again, the homeopathic salve, salicylic acid,
flame-fighting febrifuge.

Sala: inside-out "Alas," sigh
of affirmation-in-spite
-of-everything, a solemn cry
of mercy realized as grand *merci*,
universal love chosen as armor
by the jilted paramour.

Maya's cherry which secretly
bears the stone-seed of Buddhahood,
sal-*om-mani-padme-hum*-ander.

Salam/Shalom-Ander: a benediction: "Peace-to-Man;"
passionate man of peace
amidst passion's holocaust,
Word on the cross, Word in the manger.

Sa-*la-illaha-illa-allah*-mander

Salome: ekstatic maenad, tender
-hearted wetnurse & blood-crazed render,
strip-dancing the shamanic mandate,
at each of hell's seven almond-shaped gates
shedding a veil until she's translated
to the Muses' Mount Helicon
having made vulnerability
her most venerable ability,
having forged her foibles into fables,
beheading the ego—"*Sauft alle mit einander*"—
& thereby midwifing the death-in-life/life-in-death cycle.

Soolam: black stone which proves pristine dream pillow & golden
ladder to heaven & back.
Sal ammonica: piss & dung of pilgrims' camels
refined into life-promoting fertilizer, rebel's
& reveler's explosives, smelling salts to awaken consciousness.
Sacred/Taboo Untouchable, Outcast destined to cast out our sins & demons.

A la the dervish performing his turning (*sema*),
the salamander is the genius of emptiness (*sama*)
generating wings & taking flight (samara), finding
purchase in the doorway of King
Solomon's Temple.

Sa-*la-illaha-illa-allah*-mander

I am
I am that
I am that I am.
The highest cause of everything is living
within the thing itself,

verdant word as wheel & whirler of the wheel,
Dharma-chakra come full circle back to mysterious "S,"
death-tree shading Zeus' birth-cave, amphibious
alphabetic agent both of hissing demise & of plurality:
ssssSalamanderSssss.

Acknowledgments

Some of the poems herein first appeared in the following:

Big Bridge, The Burning Bush (Ireland), *The Cortland Review, Dorado, Exquisite Corpse, The Fifteen Project, The Maple Leaf Rag, Mustachioed, The North American Review, Solid Quarter, Vagabond* (L.A.), & *YAWP: A Journal of Poetry and Art.*

"YEAR OF THE ROOSTER" debuted as a letterpress broadside & "SALAMANDER; OR, SPLITTING THE WORD ASUNDER" as a letterpress chapbook, both courtesy of Verna Press.

The author is further indebted to Joseph Bienvenu & Jessa Grace Derania whose input was invaluable.

Cover drawing & author photo by Thaddeus Conti

Published by Verna Press
1120 Spain Street
New Orleans, LA 70117

To order additional copies or view other titles visit:
www.vernapress.com

Born Friday, 7 November 1969, in Worcester, Mass., David Rowe was educated at Swarthmore. His poems have appeared in *Big Bridge*, *The Cortland Review*, *Exquisite Corpse*, *The North American Review*, & on *The Moe Green Poetry Show*. He believes, along with Emerson, that every word was once a poem. Currently between addresses, he can be virtually located at www.myspace.com/davidiotraw.

An edition of 500 copies was printed at BookMobile.
The typeface is Minion Pro designed by Robert Simblach.
The name comes from the traditional naming system for type sizes,
in which minion is between nonpareil and brevier.
The book design is by Peter Anderson.